LIFE IN PRISON

LIFE IN PRISON

STANLEY "TOOKIE" WILLIAMS

WITH BARBARA COTTMAN BECNEL

PHOTOGRAPHS BY D STEVENS AND OTHERS

chronicle books · san francisco

I respectfully dedicate this book to Nelson Mandela, Angela Davis, Malcolm X, Assata Shakur, Geronimo Ji Jaga Pratt, Ramona Africa, John Africa, Leonard Peltier, Dhoruba Al-Mujahid, George Jackson, Mumia Abu-Jamal, and the countless other men, women, and youths who have to endure the hellish oppression of living behind bars.

Let this book serve as a warning to all individuals out there in society: Prison is hazardous to your mind, body, and spirit. May none of you ever have to experience the madness of incarceration.

Amani (peace),
Stanley "Tookie" Williams

Frontispiece: Here I am in 1996, standing against the wall that borders San Quentin's exercise yard for death-row inmates.

Permission for photographs is gratefully acknowledged:
Pages 2, 12, 15, 38—Stanley "Tookie" Williams and family; pages 18, 27, 35, 41, 48, 52, 68, 76—D Stevens/DSI/Zuma Press; pages 20–21—Marilyn Humphries/Impact Visuals; page 22—Jeffry Scott/Impact Visuals; page 26—Andrew Lichtenstein/Impact Visuals; page 28—C. Takagi/Impact Visuals; page 58—Corbis-Bettmann; page 64—Rosa Small

First published in 1998 by Morrow Junior Books, a division of William Morrow and Company, Inc., New York.
Published in the United States in 2001 by SeaStar Books.

Manufactured in the United States of America.

Library of Congress Cataloging-in-Publication Data is available.

ISBN 1-58717-093-0 (hardcover binding)

Distributed in Canada by Raincoast Books
9050 Shaughnessy Street, Vancouver, British Columbia V6P 6E5

1 0 9 8 7 6 5 4 3

SeaStar Books, a division of Chronicle Books LLC

Chronicle Books LLC
85 Second Street, San Francisco, California 94105

www.chroniclekids.com

CONTENTS

preface   7

foreword   9

introduction:
beware the gladiator schools   13

1. cages   17

2. a day in prison   25

3. stir-crazy   31

4. the strip search   40

5. rules   44

6. the hole   51

7. home cooking   59

8. health care   63

9. violence in prison   69

10. homesickness   77

PREFACE

by Mario Fehr

Member of the National Parliament of Switzerland

I, along with other members of the national parliament of Switzerland, have nominated Stanley "Tookie" Williams for the 2001 Nobel Peace Prize because of the extraordinary youth violence prevention and intervention work he has created from a "Condemned Row" prison cell in California's San Quentin State Prison.

Mr. Williams's journey from youth gang leader to international street peacemaker is a remarkable one. His honest self-assessment, while incarcerated, led him to encourage youth not to follow in his footsteps. His determination to keep youth out of gangs has led him to write violence prevention and gang diversion books for at-risk youth, as well as to create programs for such youth to enhance their basic literacy and computer skills, lift their self-esteem and encourage their involvement in community service.

Mr. Williams was asked by several major New York publishers to write books for adults that depicted, in coarse language and graphic scenes, stories about gang shootings, murder and the culture of young street gangsters. He refused. Instead, he wrote *Tookie Speaks Out Against Gang Violence,* an eight-book violence prevention series, for students from 5 to 10 years old. Published in 1996, the books are still being used in classrooms and libraries throughout the United States.

Since then, Mr. Williams has launched a comprehensive, international program to steer youth away from gangs, violence, drugs and imprisonment. During the past four years he has assisted in the design and content of his own educational website at http://www.tookie.com that has served youth since 1997.

He has also conceived the Internet Project for Street Peace, a peer mentoring, anti-gang and anti-crime program which links at-risk youth from the United States—via the World Wide Web— to youth in Zurich, Switzerland. In addition, there are plans to link U.S. youth to their counterparts in Johannesburg, Soweto and Cape Town, South Africa. The curriculum for the program is based on this book, *Life in Prison*, first published in 1998 and awarded two national book honors. He and Barbara Cottman Becnel, Mr. Williams's co-author, are also developing a nonprofit organization, the International Street Peace Network, which will coordinate participating Internet Project for Street Peace "technology hubs" throughout the world.

Mr. Williams is engaged in groundbreaking work. He has focused his efforts on overcoming the globalization of inner-city America's youth gang culture of street warfare. Mr. Williams is striving to eliminate this phenomenon by working with other peacemakers to develop a growing corps of youth leaders who are able to secure sustainable peace on the streets of cities and townships around the world. Thousands of emails have been sent to Mr. Williams by youth, parents, teachers, police officers and correctional officials to report how Mr. Williams's books have caused "wanna-be" gang members to stop romanticizing gang warfare, and caused those who have already joined a gang to want to get out.

Mr. Williams's international campaign to save children and support a civil society represents an unusual opportunity for a person with street-war bona fides to model reform and rehabilitation for troubled youth worldwide.

foreword

In the spring of 1971, seventeen-year-old Stanley "Tookie" Williams teamed up with Raymond Lee Washington, also seventeen, to start a street gang in South Central Los Angeles that would protect them from other neighborhood gangs. Stan and Raymond had about thirty friends who were the first members of this new group—a gang that became the notorious Crips.

Raymond was murdered in 1979 by a rival gang member. Two years later, Stan was found guilty of killing four people during two robberies. He was sent to San Quentin's death row on April 20, 1981. He has been there ever since, while he appeals his imprisonment and his death sentence.

From his prison cell, Stan has kept track of the growth of violent copycat Crips gangs across the nation and around the world: They are in forty-three states and in parts of western Africa, South Africa, Sweden, Canada, Germany, and France.

Stan now greatly regrets the violent history of the Crips. He is doing as much as he can to guide young people away from prison, and from being shot or killed. These days, Stan writes books for children of all ages that focus on the tough lessons he has learned. He wants to teach kids how to make better choices than he did. Stan has also created "Tookie's Corner," an Internet education site at www.tookie.com on the World Wide Web. There he regularly posts messages to young people that he hopes will convince them to live a life that keeps them out of prison. And Stan has an e-mail address—tookie@tookie.com—where kids can write to him if they have questions or need to communicate with someone.

I met Stan in January 1993, while I was writing a book about the history of the Crips and Bloods gangs. I needed to talk to Stan to find out how the Crips got started. After I wrote him several letters, he invited me to San Quentin to ask questions about his past as a Crips leader. During that meeting, I learned of Stan's remorse for having cofounded the Crips and discovered he wanted to make amends for that mistake—to make up for at least some of the destructiveness that had come from starting the Crips. Soon I began helping him write violence prevention books for children and develop other projects, such as "Tookie's Corner."

The way Stan and I work together is this: He writes a chapter and then dictates over the telephone what he has written. I type it into my computer and edit his work. We also talk about how a book should be written before he writes the first page. With *Life in Prison,* for example, Stan decided early on that there would be "no sugarcoating of what goes on in prison."

I agreed to work with Stan because I believe he is serious

when he says he wants to help young people experience a better life than he has had. I also believe in redemption, which means that I believe people who make mistakes—even terrible mistakes—can change their lives if they are willing to admit what they've done is wrong and work hard to rebuild their character.

From all that I've witnessed over the five years since I first met Stan, he has truly met that test of redemption.

—Barbara Cottman Becnel

INTRODUCTION

beware
the gladiator schools

I am writing from San Quentin State Prison in northern California. For seventeen years I have lived here in a small cell on death row because I was convicted of killing four people.

San Quentin is no place you'd ever want to be. It's dangerous here—you always have to watch your back. No one is safe, not even the guards. It's also lonely here. But when I was your age, I thought it would be fun to live in prison.

I first heard about what it was like to be locked up from a guy named Rock. He was the older brother of one of my friends. I was eleven years old when Rock was released from the penitentiary where he had been imprisoned for murdering his father, who used to beat up Rock's mother.

I remember sitting wide-eyed on a porch with other kids my age, listening to Rock tell stories about the years he spent in different prisons, like Soledad, Folsom, and San Quentin. He called these prisons "gladiator schools." He said prisons were places where a man could prove his toughness to

At age thirteen, I lived in South Central Los Angeles.

other men who were equally tough. I can still picture in my mind how excited Rock would get as he told us about the bloody knife fights he had in prison.

Rock was a good storyteller. Now I see that he was *too* good. His stories made prison sound like a fun place to hang out with your homeboys. Rock had most of us *wanting* to go to prison when we were old enough. I had grand thoughts of proving how tough I could be in one of those gladiator schools. And I wasn't the only one. Many of my friends felt the same way.

There were times when Rock would pull out his wallet and flash some pictures of him and his homies standing in a prison exercise yard. The men in the photos were big and buff, flexing their muscles and smiling into the camera. Iron weights and benches were in the background. I would stare at those pictures and say, "Wow. Look at all them muscles." I told myself that one day I wanted to have a big chest and large arms and have my picture taken in a prison yard.

For kids in my neighborhood, it was normal to expect to end up in prison. A lot of my homeboys' older brothers were in and out of prison. And Rock told us that there was really no difference between being in prison and being on the streets. He said that the same things that happened in prison also happened on the outside. He said that some of his homeboys would rather be in prison than in society.

This last comment was the only thing Rock said that seemed strange to me. I was looking forward to going to prison because of the dramatic tales Rock told. But even as a child I knew that at some point I'd want to get out of there.

In 1986, when this picture was taken, I was able to lift weights in prison to maintain my muscular body. Now the California Department of Corrections has removed all weights from state prisons, including San Quentin.

16

Back when I was listening to Rock, I didn't know the truth about prison life. But today, after so many years on San Quentin's death row, I know the truth. Prison is no place you want to call home.

In this book I'll tell you how it really feels to suffer a prison sentence. You'll learn that being behind bars does not prove that you're tough, nor does it prove that you're a man. Prison is a place where grown men have gone insane. It is a place where men have been killed and where some have even killed themselves.

Prison is hell. This I know.

The true stories I've written in this book are my living nightmares. My greatest hope is that the lessons the stories offer will help you make better choices than I did.

1. cages

I first arrived at San Quentin State Prison during the spring of 1981. The place looked ancient and creepy. It reminded me of a huge, shabby fortress.

When I got off the bus, I was immediately marched—with both wrists shackled to a chain wrapped around my waist—to the prison hospital for a medical checkup. When my medical checkup was completed, I was taken to The Row.

I can still remember the first time I entered the death-row cell I was told would be mine. I saw a tiny, dingy white room, nine by four feet, with steel bars, a sink, a toilet, a bunk, and a concrete floor.

I was surprised the cell was so small. To step through its barred door, I had to turn my bulky body sideways. In fact, I looked bigger than the entire cell. When I tried to do some push-ups on the floor, I couldn't do them. The gap between the wall and bunk is too narrow for my torso. So I have to do my exercises on top of the bunk, which is the widest space in the cell.

There are no tables or chairs to sit on in the cell, so I have

to invent what I need. I sleep on a mattress on the floor because the bunk—a flat rectangle of solid steel welded to four short metal legs, each bolted to the floor—is only six feet long, two and one-half feet wide. That's too small for my body. So I sleep on the floor to keep from falling off the bunk at night and hurting myself. I use the top of the bunk as a table to study, write, draw or exercise. When I need a chair, I roll up the mattress and use it for a seat. It's very uncomfortable at times, but it's this or nothing.

When I was fifteen, I had a homeboy whose mother owned a dog kennel. I used to go there to help my friend feed the dogs in their cages. There was just enough room in each cage for a dog to chase its tail. The first time I saw the cages, I realized how happy I was that I didn't have to live in them. Now I live in a cell not much bigger than those cages. Although some men here pace back and forth in their cramped areas, I refuse to do it. The pacing reminds me of the way those dogs walked around in their cages, tormented by the lack of space.

To get a feel for what it's like to live in a prison cell, test yourself. Spend ten hours—nonstop and alone—in your bathroom at home, which is probably about the size of a cell. Lock yourself inside with no more than a radio, a blanket, a book or magazine, and a couple of sandwiches. To quench your thirst, drink tap water from the sink. You can talk to family members through the door, but don't open it. Even if you're hungry, thirsty, lonely, or tired, don't open the door. When your ten hours are up, think about the fact that I have

A death-row inmate being led away in chains in San Quentin

spent approximately one hundred and fifty thousand hours in prison cells less clean and less comfortable than your bathroom.

In addition to the cramped quarters, I also had to get used to the noise in San Quentin. There is a sound-control rule here—all televisions and radios are required to have the volume switch disconnected as soon as they enter the prison.

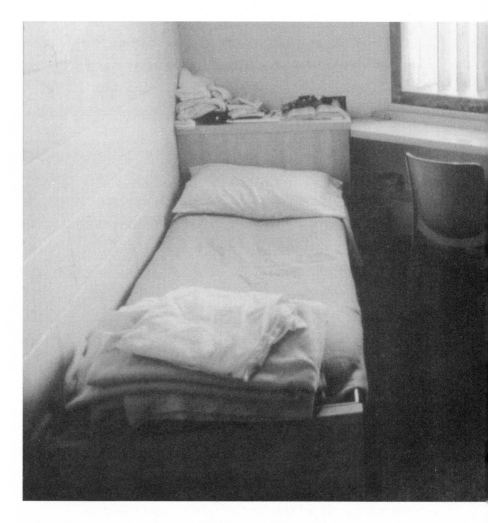

A female prisoner's cell at a jail in Boston, Massachusetts

The only way an inmate can hear his television or radio is with a set of headphones. But the sound-control rule doesn't keep it quiet during waking hours, because there are too many inmates trying to talk to each other. The building where I currently live has a total of two hundred and fifty cells. Picture about two hundred men, one man to a cell, holding different conversations at the same time. In order to be heard, they have to talk louder and louder.

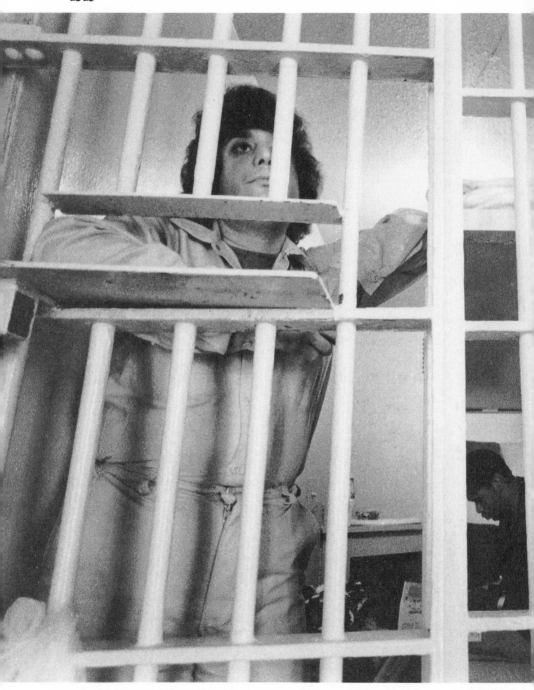

A Cuban detainee in Leavenworth Penitentiary

Sometimes the roar is so great in here it hurts your eardrums. In fact, the only time it's truly quiet is when everyone is asleep. That's why I wake up early, around 4:30 A.M., to do as much serious studying as possible before the other inmates start their day.

If the noise doesn't bother you in prison, then surely the funk—or smell—will. Some people here don't like water and will not shower. I know a guy on The Row who says that he doesn't like to shower because there are no bathtubs here. He says that until San Quentin gets some bathtubs, he will only take "birdbaths" now and then, using the sink in his cell.

Some people give up on their hygiene here in prison because they just don't care anymore. They say, "Hey, I'm on death row. Why should I take a shower? What difference does it make?"

While some inmates call the cell they live in a house, to me it's nothing like a house. If I were living in my own house, I would have the liberty to come and go as I please. I could invite a friend over whenever I wanted to and I wouldn't have to yell at my friend from behind bars in order to talk. I would have the choice every day to either shower or bathe in a bathtub. If it was cold in my house, I could turn the heater on to warm me up. Or when it became too hot, I could put the air conditioner on to cool the house. And I would have privacy. I could use the bathroom in solitude, without having to worry about guards or inmates walking by the cell and looking through the bars while I'm on the toilet.

24

I have never gotten used to that, even though I've been locked up for nearly twenty years.

Not much has changed since I first arrived at San Quentin. Space is still so tight that I often bump into the sharp edges of the bunk. I have many scars on both my knees and arms to remind me that my address is San Quentin's death row.

2. a day in prison

Day-to-day life in prison pro-
vides few opportunities to do
anything of value—or to experience peace or joy.

An inmate's day begins early in the morning, around six o'clock, with breakfast. If you're on death row, you don't get to leave your cell to eat with other prisoners. You must wait until a guard, rolling a food cart down the tier, reaches your cell and portions out your meal to you through a slot in the gate.

Inmates in the main prison eat breakfast and dinner in a large cafeteria we call a mess hall. They cannot eat lunch there, however. Instead, inmates eat brown-bag lunches in their cells or outside, on the exercise yard to which they're assigned.

After breakfast, inmates can go to the exercise yard if they choose. Guards, with handcuffs in tow, take us out to the yard beginning at seven in the morning. Once you're on the yard, you're not allowed to go back to your cell for any reason until one o'clock in the afternoon, when the exercise period is over. While on the yard, inmates can play basketball, shower, or just sit around. But it's not as much fun as it sounds, because it's a very dangerous place to be. Guards in

The "yard" at Clinton Correctional Facility in Dannemora, New York

the tower will shoot to kill an inmate if a fight breaks out. And fights happen often.

You can go outside every day while in prison. But I go to the yard only three times a week. I don't want to waste a lot of time sitting around on the exercise yard when I can be inside the cell, writing or studying.

Death-row inmates aren't permitted to work in prison, because penitentiary officials are afraid we'd try to escape.

But inmates in the main prison are expected to work. They're even penalized if they refuse to get a job. One penalty is to restrict an inmate's use of the telephone.

In prison you can work, for example, as a construction worker, janitor, cook, or gardener. But not all jobs pay a salary. And those that do pay, don't pay much. A cook and a construction worker earn the same: about a hundred dollars a month for working forty or more hours per week. That comes to approximately sixty-two cents per hour, a sum that's far below the minimum wage. Some jobs, like a beginning construction worker, pay an inmate even less: twenty dollars a month for forty hours per week of work, or about

A thirteen-year-old crack dealer nicknamed Frog lifts weights at Los Padrinos Juvenile Detention facility.

twelve cents per hour. So some inmates seek prison jobs, but many don't.

A few prisons have training programs for inmates, such as in welding and computer literacy. But that's no longer the norm. Most programs that prepare inmates for life outside of prison have been eliminated in recent years.

Inmates can spend some of their time during the day using the telephone. For the main prison population, the telephones are kept in an area outside of their cells. But death-row inmates must wait for the telephone to be brought to them. The telephone is on a cart, which is pushed down the tier by a guard. A telephone headset and cord are handed to us through the same slot as we receive

Inmates working at a license plate plant

our food. The main body of the telephone, including the dialing apparatus, remains on the cart. Each death-row cell has a telephone jack in the wall. So we plug the cord into the jack, stick our arm through the slot, and dial—collect. We can make a call only if the other party is willing to pay for it. Many friends and family members, however, put blocks on their telephones so inmates cannot charge collect calls to their numbers. So having access to a telephone a few times a week doesn't necessarily mean there will be someone willing to accept an inmate's call.

Sometimes the guards just don't feel like pushing the telephone cart, which means we don't get to use the phone that day. Not too long ago, a guard was rumored to have deliberately broken the inmate telephone. None of us inmates saw the guard do it, but this we know for sure: The cord was ripped from the cart. Our phone was out of service for nearly two weeks after that incident.

If family or friends are willing to purchase a television, radio, or books for an inmate in a state prison, then the inmate can watch TV, listen to music, or read all day in his cell. I am fortunate to have a television in my cell that my mother bought me. Federal prisons don't allow inmates to have televisions in their cells. Those inmates have to go to one of several rooms set up on certain floors to watch television.

On Sundays, inmates can worship in the prison chapel. Inmates belonging to each of the religious groups officially recognized by the prison—Catholics, Protestants, Muslims, and others—get a one-hour turn in the chapel. For many years, death-row inmates weren't allowed to go to prison church. Recently, a small chapel was built for us at San Quentin, but we can use it only once a month, and not necessarily on a Sunday. Unlike the prisoners in the main part of the prison, the death-row church has a screen that separates us from the pastor. I've chosen not to go to the prison chapel. I prefer to worship in private in the cell.

Occasionally, the boredom of prison life is interrupted for some inmates by visits from their attorneys. A very few inmates receive visits from family members, spouses, and friends.

But most inmates lie on their bunks all day, or stand around the exercise yard talking to the same people about the same topics every day, every week, every month, every year.

3. stir-crazy

Spending day after day in prison can cause strange things to happen to a person's sanity. It's easy to lose touch with reality. Some men become claustrophobic while in prison, meaning they fear being stuck in closed and narrow spaces, such as being locked in a cell. If it gets too bad, they can become stir-crazy—which means the mental pain of living in a cell for so long becomes more than they can bear.

Prisoners who are stir-crazy are insane. We call these men "J-Cats." It's slang for Category J, the official term used by prison staff to identify inmates in need of mental-health care. There are a lot of J-Cats here on death row. These men have retreated so far from reality, they don't even know they're in prison. Some of them curse at anyone who walks by their cells. Others scream and shout all night long to no one in particular. Many of them are so out of their minds that they don't take showers, comb their hair, brush their teeth, or change their clothes. They smell so bad that no one wants to be near them. Stir-crazy prisoners also urinate on themselves and smear feces all over their bodies, as well as on the walls and the floors. They may even sling human waste at you, if you're unlucky enough to be within range of their cells.

I admit that after several years here, I began to feel claustrophobic. At times I thought that I was about to go crazy. It felt like the walls were closing in on me and that if I didn't get out of the cell right then and there I would lose my mind. Sometimes my feelings of claustrophobia would last for about a minute or two. But it felt like hours. It was very frightening. I would think, Hey, wait a minute. I'm Tookie. This isn't supposed to be happening to me. But it was.

I used to get claustrophobic feelings every several months. Then, once or twice a year. Now I don't experience them at all. In fact, the last time I feared the cell was going to collapse on me was in 1989—and I had good reason to be afraid. On that day, October 17, 1989, as I sat in my cell drawing a picture, baseball's World Series was on both the television and radio. The third game was about to begin at Candlestick Park in nearby San Francisco. Excitement about the game could be heard in the voices of inmates cheering from their cells here on The Row.

I remember dropping my pencil on the floor, and at that moment, when I reached down to pick it up, the entire building began to shake. I tried to stand up, but it was hard to do—like trying to stand on top of a water bed. The motions of the floor were like the waves of an ocean.

It was an earthquake. And it was scary.

The inmates started hollering. We all felt like trapped animals. Moving as quickly as I could, I got to the front of the cell. Then I prayed that the barred door would swing open. The building was rocking so severely, I thought it might crumble. And I didn't want to be smashed under a pile of bricks. I wanted out. But there wasn't a thing I could do.

I knew that screaming would not change what was happening to me. So I just stood there, gripping the bars with all my might. I longed for the shaking to stop before San Quentin—the state's oldest in-use prison, built in 1852—collapsed. I had read that in California there would one day be an earthquake so destructive it would destroy most, if not all, of the state. With that in mind, I prepared myself for what I believed would be the end of my life.

I'll never forget how I felt that day. This is the end, I thought. I won't ever see my family again. My feelings went beyond the fear caused by claustrophobia. I didn't worry about losing my mind, because I was more concerned with remaining alive. I didn't want to die in a prison cell. But the bars remained locked. I was trapped.

The quake seemed to last forever. And there was nowhere I could run. I had never felt so helpless in my entire life. All of the big muscles I had worked so hard to develop over the years could not help me.

When the earthquake finally stopped, there was an electrical problem. So, for many hours after the quake, we had no electricity and had to sit in the dark. When the electrical power was restored, I was able to turn on the television and find out exactly how much damage the earthquake had caused. This was the worst earthquake in San Francisco since 1906.

Imagine being in your bathroom at home with the lock jammed when an earthquake hit. Picture yourself pounding on the door, screaming for your parents—for anyone—to get you out of there. Then think about how it would feel to be in that position and know that your parents were gone for the day, your neighbors were on vacation, and that no one was coming to your rescue. I'll bet you would feel abandoned, afraid, alone in the world. Most inmates carry that aching feeling inside of them virtually every single day of their incarceration.

Some of us manage to live with that pain. Some of us don't. Those of us who cannot tolerate the pain go stir-crazy.

I've kept from going stir-crazy by realizing I have only two choices: I can allow the pain to destroy me, or I can fight it. I've chosen to fight it by staying as active as possible. I write, draw, read, study, exercise, meditate, and pray. I find my greatest peace through meditation and prayer. But I'm still only tolerating a pain that never goes away.

I know several inmates who have tried to kill themselves. They say they would rather be dead than continue to live in a cell on death row.

Two inmates on The Row did kill themselves. Both were found hanging in their cells. It was hard for me to believe. For years, neither one showed any sign that he did not want to live. They saw themselves as tough guys, and they appeared to be smart and strong. They liked to exercise. Nothing seemed to trouble them, except the fact that they were on death row, which, I admit, is plenty to be troubled about.

One of them had been a Crip member for years. He had a big rep—or reputation—for himself on the streets. Back in the hood—or neighborhood—there were youngsters who looked up to him and wanted to be like him. People respected him. This man used to lift weights and was fairly

Robert Alton Harris awaits his execution on California's death row. He killed two teenagers in San Diego and was executed in 1992—the first execution in the state in more than twenty years.

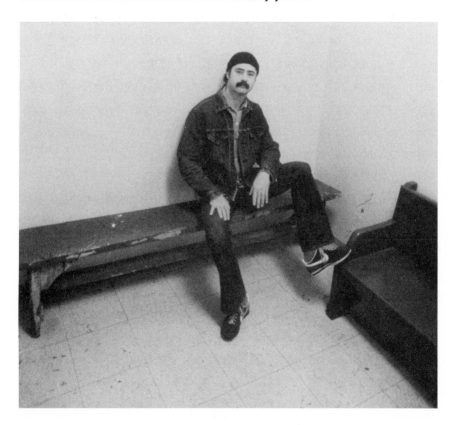

big. When he walked, he had that swagger that meant, I'm tough, so everybody had better leave me alone. Now he's dead.

Fortunately for me, thoughts of killing myself have never entered my mind. But living in prison does have a strange effect on each person here. For some people, such as J-Cats, insanity takes over. Other men, like the Crip who hanged himself, choose death.

There is much sadness behind these prison walls.

Prison life is boring—and fiercely lonely. Some inmates have relatives who will have nothing to do with them now that they're in prison. I know death-row inmates who have gone as long as ten years without visitation from any family member. Only their lawyers have come to San Quentin to see them. But when you're in prison, sometimes even your legal team won't come through for you. My attorney once went seven years without visiting me.

I'm fortunate that my mother has always been in my corner. We talk on the telephone and write to each other, and she often visits me. But there are inmates whose mothers and fathers have told them never to call or write.

Also, many of the men here used to have wives or girlfriends, as well as buddies, back home. But no more. After several months in prison, many of the people I cared about were gone from my life, too.

When you're in prison, there are no guarantees that the people you know—relatives, friends, or spouses—will remain in your life. In prison, you're out of sight and out of mind.

Years spent in a cell, by yourself and with no one to care about you, can cause an inmate to act real strange. Inmates overwhelmed by loneliness behave in ways that aren't connected to reality. If someone pays attention to them, they may start to believe that the person has romantic feelings for them. For example, a female prison professional might say only "hello" to a lonely inmate for that man to fall in love.

One of the inmates here, nicknamed Black, misunderstood a simple greeting for something more meaningful. A female nurse would from time to time ask, "How are you doing today, Black?" And because of that, Black wrote a poem for her. He would desperately try to recite the love poem during the seconds it took her to walk past his cell. First, the nurse talked to one of Black's friends on The Row about the problem she was having. She told the friend to inform Black that she was not interested in a romantic relationship with him. But Black kept writing and reciting love poetry to her. Eventually, that nurse obtained a transfer to another part of the prison to get away from Black.

Other men in prison are so crazy from their loneliness that they get angry if a female guard or nurse does not greet them or talk to them. Those inmates will yell foul language down the tiers at such women.

Loneliness is a painful feeling for everyone here. Even for me. Nothing in this cell can take away my loneliness. I can

When I'm outside on the death-row exercise yard, I like to sit by myself. It's a time to look at the sky and think.

stay as busy as ever, but the loneliness of being confined to a cell never goes away.

Fortunately for me, I have not gone stir-crazy or crazy lonely, where I've completely lost control of my actions and of my mind. And my bouts with claustrophobia have ceased. But I know better than to take for granted a relatively okay state of mind, because I know that prison life is madness.

4. the strip search

While in prison, I have witnessed—as well as personally
endured—many humiliations.
But to me the most shameful
and dehumanizing experience
is being strip-searched.

All inmates must be handcuffed and go through a strip
search each time we are escorted out of a cell or room, or
off the exercise yard. When we go to visit with our attorneys
or family members, for example, we are strip-searched before entering the visiting room, and we are strip-searched
before being returned to the cell. Even today, after being on
death row for more than seventeen years, I still have not
gotten used to being strip-searched.

Officially, there are three main reasons for conducting a
strip search: to prevent an inmate from smuggling tools or
weapons into the prison to use as part of an escape plan; to
prevent an inmate from gaining weapons to use against other
inmates or guards, or to hurt himself; and to prevent an
inmate from securing drugs or alcohol to use or to sell to
other inmates.

But most inmates believe the real reason for the strip
search is to demean an inmate or to break down his confi-

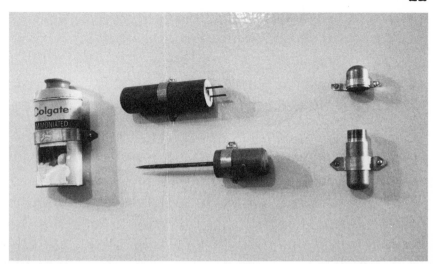

San Quentin's private display room features weapons that inmates
have manufactured over the years.

dence, so that the inmate will become easier to handle, less dangerous.

At the beginning of a strip search, the guard takes off the inmate's handcuffs and tells him to remove every piece of his clothing. If the inmate is a man, then a male guard gives the orders for the strip search. The strip-search rule applies in much the same way for women in prison. Female inmates are also strip-searched, but only by female guards.

Once a male inmate is fully undressed, he must raise his hands above his head and wiggle all of his fingers. Then he must open his mouth as wide as he can while waving his tongue from side to side and up and down as the guard peers inside to make sure nothing is being hidden in the inmate's mouth. After that, the inmate has to run his hands through his hair and brush his ears back and forth to ensure that nothing is in his hair or behind his ears. Once that's done, the inmate must lift his penis and scrotum so the guard can see if anything has been stashed underneath those parts of his body. He also has to turn all the way around, with his back to the guard, and raise each foot so the soles of his feet can be checked by the guard.

Finally, an inmate has to bend over at the waist and grab each of his butt cheeks, opening them up while coughing out loud a few times. Meanwhile, the guard, sometimes with the use of a flashlight, searches the inmate's rectum for hidden contraband, such as a knife, drugs, keys, coded messages, or anything else that might be there.

Once the strip search is completed, the inmate has to remain naked and wait for the guard to inspect each piece of the inmate's clothing, including his socks, underwear, T-shirt, pants, shirt, jacket, and tennis shoes. To make matters worse, *female* guards are often present while all this is going on. They are supposed to look away during a search, but even having them nearby makes us feel uncomfortable.

Some inmates have become so used to the strip search that it doesn't bother them anymore—it's just one more procedure they have to follow. These men go through the movements of a strip search mechanically, without emotion. Sometimes they move so fast the guard isn't able to see everything, so they have to go over the entire strip search again and again. I know a few people who had to do it four or five times before the guard was satisfied.

I know it's humiliating for *me* to be strip-searched. But I think it's also humiliating for the guards to have to conduct the searches. I couldn't stomach having to look into another person's mouth and private parts.

Think about how it would feel if neighborhoods through-out the nation were barricaded by the police to keep out weapons and drugs, and whenever you crossed those barri-cades you had to strip naked so an officer could inspect every inch of you. Anyone driving along the street could watch you being strip-searched. Now imagine having to live with this rule for the rest of your life.

That's the humiliation I face. And that's what you would face if you ever ended up in prison.

5. rules

I am sure there are times when you feel your parents are being too hard on you, that they have too many rules for you to follow. But know this: No matter how unfair you may think your parents are, or how tough you may think, their rules are, your parents' rules are nothing like the rules we are forced to abide by in prison.

There are so many rules for inmates in California prisons that they fill a large book that's 174 pages long. The book is called the *California Code of Regulations: Title 15—Crime Prevention and Corrections*. Each inmate is given a copy of this rule book so we can never claim that we broke a rule we didn't know about. Still, it's hard to keep up with the rules.

There are three reasons for this. First, there are too many rules to remember. Second, the old rules are constantly being changed. Third, new rules are always being added.

The rules in prison cover just about everything that you can think of, including:

- how much time you get to wash your body
- how long you can grow your hair
- how long you can grow your fingernails
- who can touch you during a visit, and for how long
- what type of clothes you are permitted to wear
- what kind of food you are permitted to purchase
- how long you can talk on the telephone
- what size television you can buy
- how many books you can have in your cell
- how often you can see the doctor
- how many blankets you can have for your bunk
- how many sheets of tablet paper can be mailed to you
- how many pencils are allowed in the cell, and even what size pencil you can use

Many inmates don't even bother trying to remember all of the rules. Yet they know that if they break certain rules, they are likely to end up in the Hole, or solitary confinement, which is worse than any punishment from your parents.

Cleanliness and Grooming
There are a few men here—most of them J-Cats—who refuse to bathe. They smell so bad that when you walk by their cell you want to hold your nose, but you can't because of the handcuffs that bind you. These inmates have cells cluttered with all kinds of trash, clothes—and even feces. Being that unclean is a violation of Article 5, Rule 3061, which states: "Inmates must keep themselves clean, and practice those health habits essential to the maintenance of physical and mental well-being."

Generally, the guards respond to this violation by removing the inmate from the cell and ordering him to shower. He can shower in the building or outside on the exercise yard, but he won't be allowed back into his cell until he is clean. While the inmate is cleaning himself up, the guards spray a water hose into his cell to get rid of the filth and stench.

Strict grooming rules dictate the length of our hair and our fingernails. Male prisoners are not allowed to grow their hair any longer than three inches, and sideburns are limited to one and one-half inches. Female inmates can grow their hair longer than the three-inch limit, but they must pin it up so that it doesn't hang below their shoulders. And neither male nor female prisoners are permitted to grow their fingernails more than one-quarter inch. Guards inspect us daily to make sure we comply with the rules. If we don't comply, we are severely disciplined, and may be sent to the Hole.

Showering

My guess is that your parents allow you to take as much time as you need to bathe or to shower. In prison, there is a fifteen-minute limit for inmate showers. Fifteen minutes may seem like ample time for showering, but the fact that someone dictates how long we can shower is frustrating. Each shower has a controlled timer that automatically cuts off the water after fifteen minutes. An inmate is not able to turn the water back on once the water shuts off. There have been a few times when I've been stuck with shampoo in my hair and in my eyes because the water was shut off before I was finished showering. No matter how angry I became, the guard would not turn the water back on.

Another problem with taking a shower in prison is that there is no privacy. The shower area is similar to the cells we live in. There are no doors or curtains, just steel bars, which means that people walking by can see any one of us standing in the shower naked.

Inmates being strip-searched can also see you shower. There is a cell directly across from the shower that is used to strip-search inmates on their way to another part of the prison. What typically happens is that neither inmate wants to see the other one naked. So while we say hello to each other, we avoid direct eye contact because we're embarrassed.

Visiting

The rules for visiting are some of the most annoying rules in the prison. When I go into the visiting room, I want to hug my mother, relatives, or friends as often as I want to. But the rules for visiting don't allow that. The rules are that I can hug or kiss only when I first arrive in the visiting room and again when I am preparing to leave. No kissing is allowed in between those times. If I do it anyway, the guard will walk right up to me and issue a warning. If I get caught again, the guard will end the visit, give me a write-up, or both. A write-up is when a guard prepares a formal, written complaint against an inmate because the inmate has broken a rule.

Another visiting rule is that no one can sit on your lap, not even a three-year-old son or daughter, grandchild, niece, or nephew. In the visiting room no one can braid, comb, or brush your hair. It's very humiliating to have guards watching us closely to make sure that none of us is breaking the rules by touching, or being touched, too much.

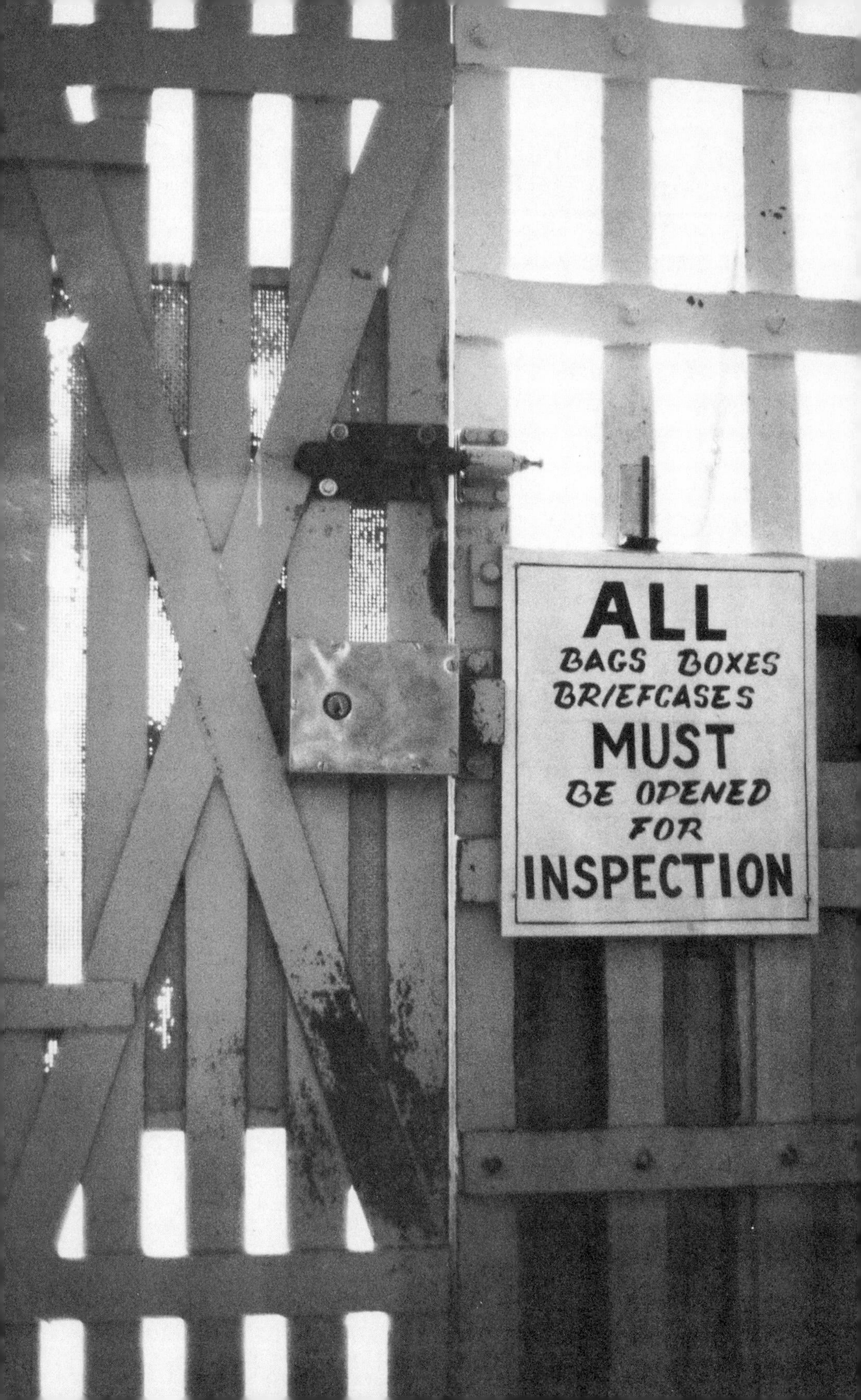
ALL
BAGS BOXES
BRIEFCASES
MUST
BE OPENED
FOR
INSPECTION

Clothing, Telephone, and Mail

In prison, there are even rules for the kind of clothing we can wear. Certain colors aren't allowed here. We can't wear red or blue shoelaces, for instance, because these are gang colors. Crips claim the color blue. Bloods like to wear red. There are rules for the amount of clothing we can have in the cell. Excess clothing is taken away from us. And when an inmate goes to the visiting room, he must wear prison-issued blue shirts and pants. No jeans are allowed.

Recently, another rule was applied for use of the telephone. There's now a fifteen-minute time limit on the telephone. Near the end of the fifteen minutes, a recorded warning that only two minutes remain interrupts your conversation. After the two minutes are up, the phone cuts off automatically, whether or not you have finished what you have to say. And don't think for one second that it's only you and whoever you're talking to on the line. Another rule is that inmate telephone conversations are monitored by a guard in a tower who, with special equipment, can hear everything.

Our mail is read by the guards to make sure that none of us is planning an escape or some other illegal activity, and that nothing illegal is being sent to us through the mail. I have had letters that took weeks, sometimes months, to reach me. And when the letters do arrive, they're often torn, or missing photographs or stamps. I can't stand knowing that some stranger is reading every letter and looking at every photograph that comes in the mail for me before I do. But as I said, there is no privacy here in prison. Everybody here hates that, but it's another prison rule. Not only does the staff read our

A sign in San Quentin warns visitors that they will be searched when they enter.

incoming mail, they also read all the letters that we send out.

The guards in prison get to know who our relatives and friends are. They find out about our family problems—and everything else—*before* we do.

Imagine your parents reading every letter you wrote before it could be mailed. Imagine them spending days, weeks, or months inspecting mail sent to you before you got to see it. Imagine what it feels like to have no privacy to communicate with your friends. In fact, for the next thirty days try living as I do.

Make an agreement with your parents that they get to control every letter you write or package you prepare for mailing, as well as every piece of mail that's sent to you. They can also send your mail whenever they get around to it, no matter how long that takes. They also have the right to throw away any mail you send or receive, without your knowledge or approval, if they don't like what you've written or what was written to you.

I won't go on and on about all the rules here, because there are too many—hundreds of rules govern prison life. Just be very, very grateful that you don't have to deal with all of the prison rules that we have to live under.

8. the hole

The Hole is a place in every prison where an inmate is sent when he gets into trouble. Most inmates fear being sent to the Hole, because in the Hole you are more isolated than ever, more locked down than before, and you have far less of everything.

Getting into trouble can involve having an argument with a guard, stealing, using or selling drugs, fighting, carrying a weapon, stabbing someone, or trying to escape. A person can also end up in the Hole if he breaks any one of the numerous prison rules, or if another inmate lies to the guards to get the person in trouble.

At San Quentin, the Hole is located in a separate building called the Adjustment Center. The Adjustment Center is quite a distance from where death-row inmates are housed. But the Hole is a place where men on death row can end up. I should know, because I've been there quite a few times. The last time, I spent close to seven years in the Hole because I was suspected by prison authorities of being involved in a gang power struggle. Several inmates, whose

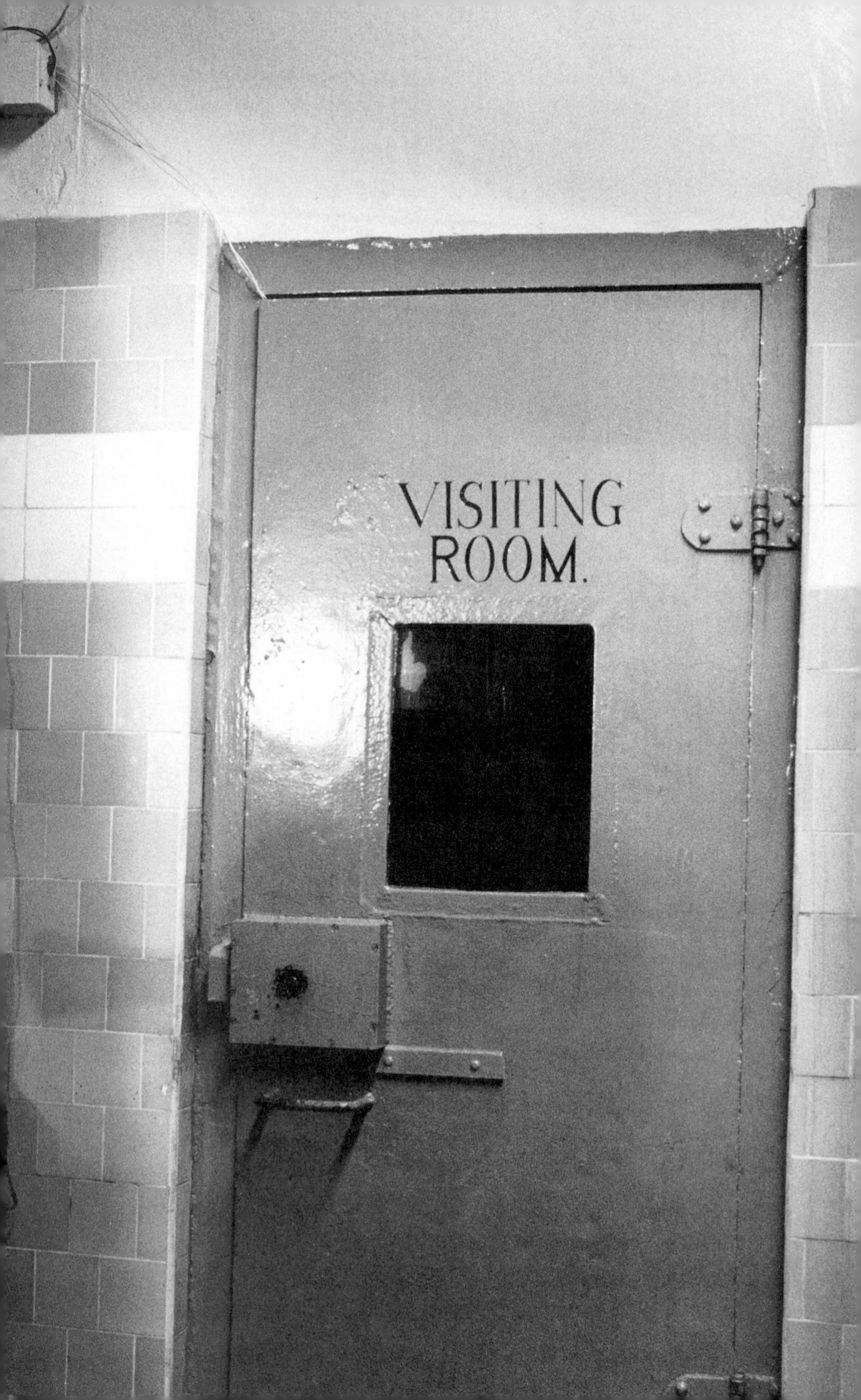
VISITING
ROOM.

identity is still a mystery to me, gave false information to prison staff members in order to get me in trouble. That's why I was locked down in the Hole. I stayed there for almost seven years because the guards were afraid of me. They feared that my release from the Hole would start a round of gang warfare in the prison. When I was released, there was no warfare.

In the Hole, a person loses most of his privileges, starting with his property. Though I had close to forty books, I was given only three of them when I was sent to the Hole. The handle of my toothbrush was shortened by half to stop me or anyone else from making a knife out of the plastic. I used to have many different kinds of pencils to draw with. But in the Hole, I could have only one pencil, and that pencil was cut real short—usually no more than two inches long, about the size of your baby finger. As for an ink pen, I was given just the filler, with no plastic or metal casing. So I made my own casing by rolling paper around the filler, then wrapping string around the paper to hold it tight.

Other restrictions include a limit on the amount of money you're allowed to spend at the prison store, called the canteen. In the Hole, thirty-five dollars is the most you can spend each month to buy food, toothpaste, deodorant, and other items from the canteen. When you're not in the Hole, you can spend more than thirty-five dollars a month at the canteen, assuming you have a family member or friend who is willing to give you that much money.

Visiting rules for people in the Hole are extremely strict. For one thing, an inmate is not allowed to have physical con-

Before entering the visiting area, San Quentin inmates see this sign.

tact with his visitors. When I was in the Hole, I wasn't able to hug or touch my mother or anyone else who came to visit. I couldn't touch them because I was locked in a booth. That booth contained a stool to sit on and a telephone that allowed me to talk to my visitors as we looked at each other through a glass window.

In the Hole, you're allowed only two visits per week, and only on separate days—one visit for each day. Other inmates can get up to four days' worth of visits each week, and up to six hours per visit. When you're in the Hole, you're lucky to get a two-hour visit.

If the visiting room for the Hole is crowded, then your visit will be cut to one hour because of the shortage of booths. San Quentin has only thirteen booths to serve the visitors of the more than one hundred inmates who are in the Hole on any given day. There were times when friends or family members traveled nearly five hundred miles to visit with me for an hour. And sometimes they came that far and weren't able to see me at all, because the visiting room was simply too crowded. Time ran out before a booth became available.

So even one hour with your family member is precious when you're in the Hole, and it's painful to have the visit come to an end. I remember how I would dread seeing the guard walk up to the booth to tell me it was over.

I also hated that, when it was time to go, my mother and other family members would have to watch me stand up, place my hands and wrists behind my back, and then push them through a narrow slot cut into the steel door at the rear of the booth for a guard to handcuff. The last thing my family would see was me being led away by the guards, my hands locked together behind me and flapping up and down as I tried to wave good-bye.

Although your family can visit you while you're in the Hole, you're not allowed to talk to them on the phone. The only time that anyone in the Hole can use the telephone is in the case of an emergency, meaning a death in the family or a legal call to an attorney. In the Hole, there is only one way to communicate regularly with someone you care about: writing letters. But in addition to the usual delays, when I was in the Hole, I could hear men complaining daily that their mail had been tampered with. So you can't always rely on the mail when you're in the Hole.

At any time there can be a massive search of cells in the entire building that houses the Hole. The searches are done in a very careful manner. Everything inside each cell is checked. That means the guards look inside every container, bag, book, letter, and light switch. They look under the bunk and inside the toilet, and they inspect the bars to make sure no one is trying to cut them and get out of the cell. Before checking the cell, the guards strip-search us. Then we are escorted outside of the cell by the guards. With our wrists handcuffed behind our backs *and* to one of the steel bars, we stand in a line, wearing only a pair of white boxer shorts and shower slippers, or thongs.

Another time we wear our boxer shorts is when we go to the Committee. We can meet with the Committee—a small group of prison staff who determine whether we can get out of the Hole—once every ninety days, until they finally release us from the Hole. These Committee members are, of course, fully dressed when we visit them in our underwear, seeking to be let out of the Hole. We are made to undress supposedly because it assures the guards that we are not hiding any weapons in our clothes. But it's another humiliating experience for anyone living in the Hole.

When we're in the Hole, we can go to the exercise yard only three days a week, not seven. There are three different exercise yards; usually the particular yard an inmate goes to is determined by his race or gang affiliation, and by whether staff members believe he can get along with the other men on the yard he wants to go to.

When we go to an exercise yard, we are made to dress, again, in white boxers and tennis shoes, and we are strip-searched twice—once inside of the cell where we live, then a second time in the holding cell before we go outside. When the yard time is over, we are again searched in the holding cell, prior to returning to our cells.

When we're on the yard, we wear the same outfit—white boxers and tennis shoes—regardless of whether the sun is shining or it's extremely cold or rainy.

In the Hole, J-Cats are at their worst. A few of them are even crazy enough to attack a guard—or other inmates—if they have the chance. Usually, though, J-Cats end up getting themselves hurt, especially when they're out on one of the exercise yards.

I remember one J-Cat who walked up to a guy he didn't even know and socked the man in the back of his head.

When the smoke cleared, the J-Cat was beaten up so badly he had to be carried off the yard.

There are some people who aren't crazy but who behave like J-Cats. They're called Cell Soldiers. They talk loudly, as if they intend to do something to you, but they won't, because they never leave their cell. You can find Cell Soldiers in the Hole, on death row, and in the main prison population. They'll challenge others to a fight, knowing that they won't ever go outside to the yard. Or they'll throw things on inmates passing their cells, knowing that they can't get beaten up.

Most of the men in the Hole are thought by prison staff to be the worst of the worst, because they're considered extremely violent and hard-hearted. Still, I don't know one man who did not want to get out of the Hole. Sure, there were some who would talk about how they didn't care if they had to do all of their time in the Hole. But in the back of their minds, they were hoping and praying that they would get out of the Hole as soon as possible. I know that's what I was doing. Wouldn't you?

7. home cooking

Do you remember any delicious meals that you've enjoyed with your family? I can. My family is from Louisiana, and our meals tended to be very spicy. Some of the dishes my mother prepared that I especially liked were okra-seafood gumbo, fish croquette, and stuffed crab.

Since I've been in prison, I haven't had one meal that I care to remember. In fact, I try to forget them all. No meal here can compare to home cooking. To eat the food here, I have to pour a lot of hot sauce all over it to smother the nasty taste. It's awful.

The worst meal I can recall having here was something called salmon loaf. As far as I could tell, it was made of bread, salmon, and some other types of seasoning. It looked like bread pudding with bits of fish sprinkled in it. It smelled like castor oil, and it tasted worse than that. There are fifty-four men on each floor of the prison, and whenever the food cart arrived on my floor with salmon loaf, no more than three out of the fifty-four would eat the stuff.

The dining area at a high-security prison on Rock Quarry, Bufford, Georgia

In prison, there's a different meal for each day of the week, but that menu is repeated every week of every month of every year. So whatever is served on Monday is served virtually every Monday of the year, and the same is true of the other six days of the week. On the rare days that the menu varies, we don't get to try a new dish. What happens is that Monday's meal, for example, may for some reason be switched with Tuesday's meal.

The typical prison breakfast menu changes each day. It ranges from rock-hard waffles to scrambled or hard-boiled eggs, along with bacon, potatoes or grits, and ground beef sauce over rice. There's also bread, fruit, milk, and coffee. For lunch, the guards pass out a paper bag filled with an apple, a banana, or raisins; a small bag of chips; several cookies; four slices of white bread; two slices of bologna; a small bag of presweetened Kool-Aid; and two packets of mustard or mayonnaise. Our dinners alternate between chicken, liver, beef stew, veal, spaghetti, and fish. The vegetables we're served alternate as well. We get corn, carrots, green peas or beans, cabbage, cucumbers, squash, and salads. Desserts include chocolate, vanilla, lemon, or strawberry cake and apple or cherry pie. Sometimes we get cookies.

Although what I've listed may sound appetizing, none of it is. All we ever get is slop. In fact, I take multivitamins twice a day, since I'm not sure that I can get enough nutrients from the awful food here.

In the seventeen years that I've been here, the food has gone from bad to very bad. Also, there's no guaranteed time to eat breakfast, lunch, or dinner in prison. In general, breakfast arrives at about six in the morning, we get a bag lunch at eleven, and dinner comes after four. But we never know for sure. The food cart gets here when it gets here. If a person is hungry and the cart is late, he has no choice but to deal with his hunger.

After completing a meal, an inmate might still be hungry, because the portions served to us are so small. The paper trays we eat off of are similar to the trays in a school cafeteria—only smaller. We eat with plastic forks and spoons, which break very easily. If you need sugar, salt, or pepper, the guard will give you two tiny packets of each. Even the milk carton we get here is smaller than the standard size, and it's low-fat and tastes watered-down.

There are no second helpings in prison, so the first serving will have to do. This is not like home, where a person can eat as much as he or she wants to.

Because the food in prison is so terrible, I rarely eat from the cart. When I do, I get only the vegetables and fruit. Instead, I order food products once a month from the canteen. We aren't allowed to go to the store and pick out the food we want, though. Instead, we have to fill out a form for the guard to process, then wait two weeks for the food to be delivered to the cell.

I buy a lot of soups, hot sauce, and mixed vegetables from the canteen—that's how I survive here. But not everybody in prison is able to go to the canteen, because they don't have money. None of us on death row is permitted to work at a prison job, so we have to depend on relatives, friends, or spouses to send us money. Without financial help from the outside, nobody on death row would get to go to the canteen.

Every three months we are allowed to receive a food package mailed to us from our relatives or friends. The package cannot weigh more than thirty pounds. Though a thirty-pound food package may seem like a lot, it doesn't last that long. Somebody has to really care about you to put together a food package. And there are not many inmates—particularly death-row inmates—who have someone willing to take the time and to spend the money on a thirty-pound food package. So when someone receives a package, that inmate will often share what he has with other, less fortunate inmates. That's why a thirty-pound food package doesn't go far.

In prison, we suffer in many ways. I miss being able to eat a wide variety of foods. I miss being able to drink an ice-cold soda. I miss being able to use as much salt and pepper as I choose. I miss being able to sit down at the table with my family to eat a Thanksgiving dinner.

8. health care

It's 2:00 a.m. and your stomach hurts so much that you wake up. Although you want to get out of bed and tell your parents how you feel, the pain forces you to stay there. Fortunately, your parents hear your moans and groans. They rush into your bedroom and discover you're sick. They decide to take you to the emergency room at the local hospital. Once there, the doctor checks you out and finds that it was something you ate earlier that is causing your stomach pain. The doctor gives you some medicine—right then and there. By the time you return home, you're feeling better.

In prison, things don't happen that fast. There are thousands of men here. In order to see the doctor, an inmate has to have his name placed on the list with other inmates who need medical attention. Sick call is twice a week. Sometimes

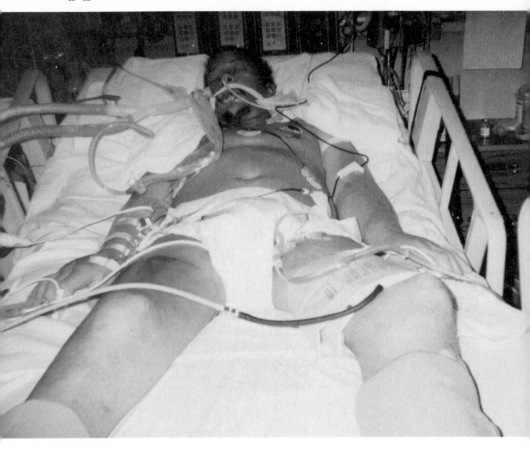

An inmate at a Los Angeles County jail felt sick for weeks but was given only aspirin by the guards. He fell into a coma and was sent to a Los Angeles hospital.

it takes days, or even weeks, before an inmate can see a doctor, because the list is full. If an inmate doesn't make it on the list for either of the weekly sick call days, then he has to try again the following week.

There is no quick relief if you catch a cold in here, and

catching a cold in prison is very easy to do. There are thousands of men living in close quarters in prison, so when one or two inmates catch a cold, usually just about everybody else will get sick. And we have no medicine cabinets or drugstores to go to for cough syrup or a couple of aspirins. When the doctor is finally ready to see us, our names are called over the loudspeaker. Then we are escorted to one of several cells in front of a tiny room, which is where the doctor and nurse do the checkup. We remain handcuffed while the doctor undertakes the examination.

My experience has been that, by then, so much time has passed the illness may have already healed itself.

Because of a recent new rule, prison health-care services are no longer free. Each sick call visit to the prison doctor costs an inmate five dollars, and quite a few medications have to be bought by inmates from the prison's canteen—which involves filling out a form and waiting, often a day or more, for the medication to be delivered to the cell.

Many of the same medical problems that occur in society also exist in prison. There are some inmates here with AIDS, a disease that weakens the immune system. I have a close friend on death row who has diabetes, which means his body does not process sugar very well. We call this man Ghetto. Because of Ghetto's muscular body, no one would think he is a diabetic and has to take insulin shots twice a day. But there have been plenty of times when his blood sugar was real low, causing him to pass out and fall to the ground. After being around him for so many years, most of us can tell when he is about to lose consciousness. Usually beads of sweat will appear on his forehead, or he will get a dazed look and have trouble walking.

Once when I was on the exercise yard doing chin-ups, Ghetto fell flat on his face, cutting a small gash in his forehead and scratching his eyeglasses. Another inmate and I placed him on a stretcher so that the guards could take him to the hospital. Because Ghetto collapsed on the exercise yard, where he could be seen, we were able to notify a guard and get him immediate help. That's what we do when someone gets sick or is injured outside of his cell. If Ghetto had been in his cell, then a somewhat different procedure would have taken place, a procedure that may or may not have produced fast results.

In prison, when someone becomes real sick in his cell, he has to holler "Man down" and shout out his cell number to receive help from the guards. Once the "Man down" call has been acknowledged, then several guards will rush up to the cell with a gurney, if need be. The inmate will be handcuffed and taken to the prison clinic. If the health problem is too serious for the prison hospital to handle, then the inmate is sent to a specific hospital on the outside.

If an inmate is too sick to holler "Man down" but is able to get word to his neighbor in the cell next to him, that person will holler "Man down" and other inmates along the tier will join in, hollering "Man down" until the guards respond. But if an inmate is too sick to let someone know he needs help, he will have to hope a guard happens by his cell and notices that he is ill. Or an inmate has to pray that he is still conscious by the next hourly count, when guards check all the cells to make sure we're there. A special count happens at four in the afternoon. The prison rule states that at that time every inmate must have his cell lights on and stop what he's doing to stand up as the guard passes down the tier. At that time the guard is supposed to make sure each inmate is okay, not sick or dead.

Imagine having to live with the knowledge that no matter how sick you are, you can never count on getting the medical attention that you need right away, not even an aspirin tablet. Think about how it feels to rely on prison guards, instead of people who love you, like your parents, to help you in a life-or-death health situation. And imagine being haunted by the fear that you will die alone in a prison cell because a guard didn't get there in time.

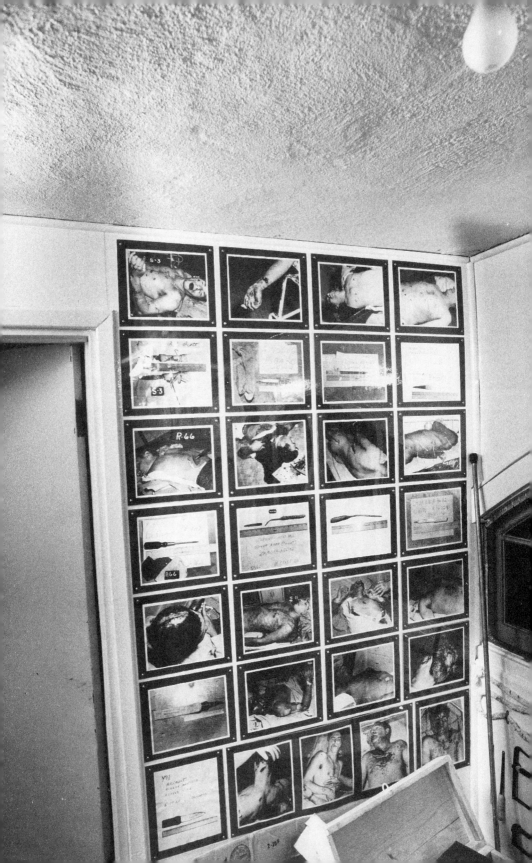

5. violence in prison

In prison, violence is like an active volcano—it can erupt at any time. Violence can come from someone you hardly know, or even from someone who is very close to you. You can have a friend today, and tomorrow he can become your number-one enemy. It's crazy in here.

Imagine knowing someone for many years, someone you grew up with and went to elementary school with. You and he have eaten meals at each other's homes. You know each other's parents. In prison, that same friend can turn against you and try his best to hurt you for all sorts of reasons. Your friend might think you're lying to him, cheating him, or stealing from him. He might attack you for owing him money for a gambling debt, or for hanging out with the wrong kind of person—a known snitch or a rival gang member, for instance.

I remember two inmates who had been close friends until one day they suddenly became bitter enemies. Both belonged to the same gang in prison. One of them was given an order by his gang but refused to follow it. The friend of

A San Quentin private display room exhibits a gruesome reminder of the violence that exists between inmates. The wall contains the photographs of those who died in the prison.

the inmate was then instructed to punish him for not following the order. When he tried to impose the punishment, the friendship between the two men ended.

There have also been times when an inmate has attacked his own flesh-and-blood relative in here. Nobody is ever safe behind these walls.

In prison, violence is always close—you can't get away from it. It takes place in closed-in areas where there are always one or more armed guards on a high-gun rail above our heads, ready to shoot to kill if we don't stop fighting or stabbing one another. In fact, inmates getting shot at or killed is a sight that most men in prison see regularly.

A few years ago, I saw a homeboy get shot in the leg by a guard during a fight with another inmate on the exercise yard. The bullet damaged his leg so badly that the doctors had to amputate it. Now he has an artificial leg and walks with a terrible limp.

In prison, a person can lose more than a leg during a fist-fight. He can lose his life if he doesn't see the guard aiming a rifle at him, or if a friend doesn't pull him out of the way in time—an act of loyalty that you can't always count on. Usually when shots are being fired, all the inmates are busy looking out for themselves and running for cover to avoid being hit by a bullet. Here, a bullet can be meant for one person but end up hitting or killing somebody else.

No one here really wants to be killed. We don't wake up in the morning and say, "Well, this is a fine day for dying." Still, there are times during a heated fight with knives (put together in prison) when no one cares about stopping, even when shots are being fired. As a rule, here in prison, the guards are supposed to fire a warning shot. But there have been many times when there weren't any warning shots. This often depends upon who you are and if you have caused some problems for the guards. You can even end up becoming a known target for some guards who have a grudge against you.

Some of us have had run-ins with the guards. I, for one, have had physical and verbal fights with them. But the guards have many harsh ways to deal with us in here. One way is with a short rifle that looks like a sawed-off shotgun. We call it Big Bertha. It shoots rubber bullets. I know from personal experience that when that rubber bullet hits you, it will make you bend over and hug yourself in pain.

I have heard with my own ears the yelling of grown men who have been hit by one of those rubber bullets. They sounded like screaming kids on a roller coaster. I have heard men give up as soon as they saw a guard holding Big Bertha. The force of the rubber bullet can drop a man to his knees or knock him up against a wall. The feeling is similar to being hit on the body with a sledgehammer. I have a friend who used to battle with the guards on almost a daily basis. He would be attacked by Big Bertha again and again. He has been hit with the rubber bullet more times than anyone I know. He still talks about how dangerous that bullet is.

Then there is the taser gun, which shoots a high voltage of electricity into your body. That, too, will drop anybody. Although I've never been stung by one, I do know quite a few inmates who have been shot at with a taser gun when they refused to allow guards to handcuff them, or when they wouldn't come out of the cell. Some of them were knocked out by the taser. They say the pain was like nothing they had ever felt. I believe them.

Sometimes when an inmate refuses to cuff-up, or be handcuffed, and come out of the cell, the guards—dressed in riot-type clothing, carrying large shields to protect themselves—rush in on that inmate. Sure, some of us can fight one, two, or maybe three guards charging into the cell. But usually the guards keep coming at you in waves, more and more of them, until you get tired and aren't able to fight anymore. That's when it's their turn to do whatever is necessary to get you out of the cell.

We refuse to cooperate with the guards for a lot of reasons. Sometimes we're angry about being locked up, about being stuck in the Hole, or about facing execution by the state. At other times, we make a decision to stand up for a cause that we believe in, like not having to cut our hair, even if it means being hit by Big Bertha, the taser gun, or whatever else the guards might use against us.

I'm sure you are aware that racial violence happens out there in society. Well, there is also racial violence in prison among the black, white, and Latino inmates. You would think that everybody in here would be more concerned with getting out of prison than with the race of another inmate. But that isn't so. There are dangerous race wars in prison. Guards sometimes get involved, too. Some of them are either openly or secretively racist. Those guards often pit racist inmates against other inmates, creating a conflict that ignites an all-out racial war. It doesn't take much persuasion to convince a foolish inmate to set someone up, through acts of violence or cell soldiering. So you always have to watch your back in here, while hoping that your friends are doing the same.

Although some prisons are still called gladiator schools, don't let that name fool you. In gladiator schools of the past, inmates had face-to-face fights. Nowadays, if your back is turned and you have enemies, you can find a knife shoved deep into your spine or the back of your neck.

We have what are called drive-bys in here, but they're not the kind you have out there in society. These drive-bys don't involve cars and guns but rather swift feet and sharp knives. On the exercise yard, the shower is next to the toilets. There is a brick wall about waist high surrounding this area of showers and toilets. Everyone on the yard can see you—and get to you. So you can be taking a shower or using the toilet on the exercise yard when some nut rushes up behind you, sticks you with a knife, and takes off running, throwing the knife away as he goes.

Imagine having to look over your shoulder all day long, every day, to protect yourself from being hurt. Well, that's the way it is in prison. If you do have a friend in prison with you, you had better make sure he is someone you can trust, because your life may depend upon it. I have known inmates who were stabbed while standing with their so-called friends. Instead of helping these inmates, the friends ran off and left them to bleed to death.

Prison is a particularly dangerous place for first-time inmates. When they arrive here, they don't have the slightest idea about what can happen to them, or about what the older inmates can make them do. No matter what their reputation was on the street, they are very likely to end up being a flunky for some other inmate who is stronger and more vicious, or who has such a long sentence he feels that he has nothing to lose. Out of fear, a flunky will do nearly anything he is ordered to do by another inmate.

Some young inmates will be made to do some pretty terrible things, worse than being a flunky. Some young men are forced to serve the sexual needs of older, tougher inmates.

Yes, there are things that can happen to a person in prison that are more frightening than your most horrific nightmare.

In here, a threat can be just as dangerous as a knife or a fist. Some men have become so scared of threats that they end up killing themselves just to avoid facing whatever they think *might* happen to them. Other inmates who are afraid of threats of violence choose to stay in their cells, imposing solitary confinement on themselves.

I know a man who was so scared of threats that his body shook, his teeth chattered, and his lips turned a pale, nearly white color. One other man I know began to stutter for the first time in his life, out of fear that he would be killed. Some men even defecate or urinate on themselves because they so fear becoming a victim themselves.

Here, violence can touch anyone, not just the men behind bars. Guards have been attacked or killed in prison as well. There are many guards who are afraid. Some guards try to act real tough to overcome their fear, because they know that if they show any sign of weakness while they're in prison, *somebody* will use it against them.

As I said earlier, nobody in prison is safe. I don't care how tough you may think you are. Anyone in prison can get attacked. Peace is promised to no one in here. But violence is promised to everyone.

The view from a guard's perspective of the recreation yard for the
Adjustment Center inmate population at San Quentin

10. homesickness

I have been locked up nearly twenty years, and every day of my incarceration I have been homesick.

Homesickness is probably what you felt the first night you spent away from home, when you stayed at a friend's house or attended summer camp. Did you start missing home right away? Did you feel sad about not being in *your* room under *your* covers in *your* bed? Those are some of the things you feel when you're homesick. I'm sure that once you returned home, those bad feelings went away.

Unlike you, I can't go home and relieve my homesickness. I can't forget about the life I once lived outside of prison. And I can't forget my memories. But worst of all is knowing that there is no cure for my homesickness.

My homesickness even makes me feel sick to my stomach. The deep longing that I have to be at home with my relatives and friends actually hurts me physically. It's a painful ache that will not go away.

Though I can hide my homesickness from others in here, and I do hide it, I've learned that I cannot hide the pain of homesickness from myself. And that's why of all the reasons there are to hate being in prison—the tiny cagelike cell, the struggle to stay sane, the tasteless food and humiliating strip searches, the unending list of rules, the ever-present violence—for me, the worst thing about prison has been my almost-twenty-year bout with homesickness.

Years ago, there were times when I became so homesick I felt like hollering, "Okay. This joke has gone far enough. Now let me out of here right now so that I can go home." But I knew all too well that where I was was real, and that no one was going to open the gate and allow me to leave.

There are many things that I miss while in prison. Experiences in daily life that are no big deal to you out there in society are a big deal to me and the other inmates in here. How many times, for example, have you passed a garden of beautiful flowers? Did you stop and smell them? Can you remember how grass feels? I can't. There are no flowers, grass, or dirt in the part of the prison where I have to live, only steel bars and concrete. So I miss seeing, smelling, and touching flowers, grass, and even dirt.

I miss being able to go for a walk whenever I feel like it. I also miss going to the beach, or to the movie theater. There are no restaurants in prison, so I can't go to one, not even a fast-food place. I can't even go to the local library to check out a book, or to a bookstore to buy one.

Do you have a pet? What kind of pet do you have? Is it a dog, cat, fish, or bird? From time to time when I'm on the exercise yard, I will see different kinds of birds flying high in the sky. But that's as close as I can get to an animal in prison, unless it's a rodent running past my cell on its way down the tier. I would like to have a pet, but I can't. None of us here can have one.

One of the reasons I don't like looking out the cell's dirty window at the boats that sail by is that it reminds me of home. When I was a kid, I used to take long walks by myself along the Santa Monica beach and stare at the ocean for hours. I also don't like looking out that window because I begin to daydream about the what-ifs: What if I hadn't gotten expelled from high school? What if I hadn't cofounded the Crips? What if I hadn't ended up on death row? Would I have owned a boat? Would I have learned to sail? That kind of thinking makes me sad, makes me long to be home and starting my life over again.

Right now, as you read this, you are probably free from incarceration. You may be unhappy at home and you may feel that you don't have a lot of choices in your life. But you still have the freedom to live a full life. As an inmate, especially a death-row inmate, my life is very limited. There are so many things that I will never be able to do, so much that I will never see. The pain of knowing this is something I have had to endure my entire prison term.

Being burdened with homesickness while in prison is one of the worst feelings you would ever want to experience. So stay out of this place by staying out of trouble, by making better choices than I did.

Strive to do well in school—don't drop out or get kicked out, which is what happened to me. Learn as much as you can about your culture, the history of the community where you live, technology, politics, economics, and morality. I waited until I was in prison to study these topics. You can do it right now. And use what you've learned to join with your friends and come up with ideas to make your neighborhood a better and safer place to live.

If there are times when you are tempted to commit a crime, to go against what you know is right to prove you're tough or cool, don't do it. And don't be fooled by people like Rock, who may tell you how much fun it is to be in prison. Just remember what I have told you, which is the truth about what life in prison is really like—and stay out of here. Do not follow in my footsteps.